I0407615

Social Collapse Survival Guide

by Tristan Trubble

Published in USA by:

Tristan Trubble
P.O BOX #9
Boynton Beach
FL 33425

© Copyright 2017

ISBN-13: 978-1546528159
ISBN-10: 1546528156

ALL RIGHTS RESERVED. No part of this publication may be reproduced or transmitted in any form whatsoever, electronic, or mechanical, including photocopying, recording, or by any informational storage or retrieval system without express written, dated and signed permission from the author.

Table of Contents

Introduction

How do you define "social collapse?" Answers to this question vary across the board. The variations often depend on who is answering the question, opinion on the matter of what constitutes "collapse" is directly related to each individual's lifestyle, education, social status, and numerous other aspects that factor into the development of individual opinion.

Social collapse scenarios can range from brief, violent, temporary, lapses in what we consider the status quo, or they can be prolonged events that last for weeks, months, or years. Social collapse can result from man-made or natural disasters. In a nutshell, social collapse is the absence of Rule of Law, when law and order is temporarily abandoned in the face of disorder. Civil unrest, protests that escalate into riots, the looting of local businesses after a natural disaster; these are all examples of social collapse on a small, regional scale. These small, regional collapses have the potential to develop into battlefields and war zones.

Throughout world history, social collapse is ubiquitous and pervasive, so much so that it's become an accepted part of our world. Historically, empires rise and fall like the tides of the ocean. The ancient Egyptians, so far ahead of their time, experienced social collapse and eventually became a footnote in history. The same can be said about the ancient Romans, Greeks and the Persian Empire of Xerxes. Each one of these empires were considered the epicenter of civilization, only to collapse, their remains, their artifacts laid out for tourists like an open tomb.

History shows humans are just as hazardous as nature, when it comes to disaster; man-made social collapse in Nazi Germany. WWII Germany was a budding empire unsatisfied with the demographics of Europe. They decided that implementing genocide on an enormous scale was the best course of action. The social collapse conditions, promoted by the Nazi regime, resulted in the formation of an alliance among international entities to remove the dictatorship and rebuild society for the benefit of all ethnicities involved.

As this is being written, several countries in the Middle East are experiencing devastating conditions of social collapse, or are teetering on the threshold of war. Iraq and Afghanistan are just coming out of war with the United States, and although all American troops have started to withdraw, violence, terrorist attacks and war are still being waged in both countries. Libya continues to be a hot topic of conversation, and Syria is in the midst of a civil war that has decimated the country and the population.

America herself is no stranger to social collapse conditions, both historically and in modern times. The American Revolution, the American Civil War, and the Great Depression are some early examples of social collapse in this country, while the 2008 recession and subsequent high unemployment is a current threat of how easy it might be for America to spiral into chaos.

Detroit, Michigan serves as a shining example of this. Motown, once considered the epicenter of American automotive ingenuity, boasted almost two million residents during its heyday. Having filed for bankruptcy, the city now claims less than 750,000 residents. Massive tracts of empty houses dot the landscape, old buildings are left to crumble in the heart of the city, and essential services are seriously understaffed and overworked. Law enforcement agencies are undermanned, which results in a spike in criminal activity. Detroit's big and small businesses are closing on a daily basis, without providing employees prior notification in order for them to prepare for job loss. The sky-rocketing unemployment rates require people to file for a handout while searching for a new job in an area where the job market is shrinking exponentially. This type of social collapse is also man-made. Illegal activities, corruption, and terrible economic planning, carried out by the city's elected officials has had devastating consequences city-wide. The overall impact this will have on the future of Detroit remains to be seen. Without a resourceful bail-out plan in place, Detroit could very likely end up being a hollow husk of a once prosperous city. Should that happen, the impact from the city's corpse could bleed across the entire state.

We also witness small-scale social collapse here in America on a regular basis. The Boston Marathon bombing is an example of just such an insular collapse, one that impacts small numbers of US citizens in a big way, and the rest of us in small ways. When this tragic event occurred, panic, chaos, and confusion were heavy in the air. All walks of life were affected – cops, first responders, MSM agencies, and even the White House administration, all presented different information regarding the event, which threw intelligence into turmoil. The days that followed the Boston bombing involved mesmerizing screenshots and videos of the complete and total lockdown of a suburb of Boston, while thousands of militarized law enforcement agencies poured through the area. It was, in fact, a Martial Law situation in which residents were given specific instructions to STAY INSIDE. The regional residents were greeted at their doors by heavily armed law enforcement personnel, often without due process. The rights of innocent citizens were overlooked as the manhunt for one of the 'suspected' bombers was performed at the business end of an automatic assault rifle.

The face of this once great nation can't offer any insight or transparency about these events. This dishonesty by our government has resulted in the forming of activist groups. Some groups and organizations are gearing up to host massive marches and protests, which could ultimately result in the development of a larger social collapse scenario.

We also see social chaos stemming from the collapse of national currency, as in the recent case with Greece. Some predict this same type of social collapse for America in the very near future. Our current currency system is ripe with fraud and corruption, as it has been since the inception of the Federal Reserve and the IRS. A number of economic leaders in this country have forewarned the world that a monumental economic collapse is overdue. Given the fact that America functions on a fiat currency system, continues to spend and borrow excessively from international banks, and prints money as needed without any backing of value, it isn't hard to envision America falling into serious economic collapse, which has the potential to morph into nationwide civil unrest, and the eventual collapse of our society.

The fact that America polices the world doesn't help matters either. Recent pollings indicate that the average American citizen is against prolonged involvement in Syria. Depending on where we get our news, and what we choose to believe, some international experts insist that prolonged American engagement in the Syrian situation has the potential for launching WWIII.

Here in America, concerns grow over our own government's domestic policies. While the importance of this scandal has been moved to the back burner, the DHS has purchased billions of rounds of ammunition, and several previously unarmed federal agencies have begun training and issuing weapons to their agents to enforce laws not yet accepted by the general population. Several conspiracies also link these activities to the existence of FEMA camps which are popping up all over the country. These camps do exist and have the harrowing appearance of modern day death camps, euphemistically labeled "Residential Relocation Centers." Conclusions are then drawn by some that the American government has covert plans to enslave the population. Theories of what the government has in store range from implementing Agenda

21 on a national scale to possible genocide.

Though we've covered man-made social collapse, we haven't even touched on the natural disasters that occur across the globe. These types of events easily bring about social collapse. They have a disastrous economic effect and a devastating societal impact. Not only are the effects of wide-scale natural disasters themselves overwhelming, but the criminal activities rampant in the aftermath also induce societal collapse.

Rioting, looting, and an increase in assault, rape, and murder are all potential threats after a natural disaster. Debris removal and rebuilding scams are also commonplace. Lack of necessities and essentials are evident within a few hours of a massive natural disaster, such as Hurricane Katrina. Ineffective government intervention also contributes to social collapse during the aftermath of natural disasters of this magnitude. The shelters the government sets up are often overcrowded and understaffed. The Rule of Law is almost non-existent in these situations, as the few law enforcement personnel available are tasked with attending to the urban areas. Medical services are also understaffed and normally supplies are insufficient to assist everyone in need. This is really just the tip of the iceberg when it comes to the history of social collapse, modern-day social collapse, and what constitutes social collapse in general. Now that we know what social collapse is and what it looks like, on to the next question: how do we survive it?

Chapter 1:
Where to Begin

Your personal social collapse survival plan should be tailored to your current living conditions. There isn't a single universal solution for everyone. People that live in large metropolitan areas will have a drastically different battle plan in place than those living in a rural region, where their closest neighbor is several miles away. The survival plan for individuals living in suburban areas might be a mix between the two extremes, adopting aspects both rural and metropolitan.

The landscape of the region in which you live will also play an important role in determining the social collapse survival plan you put in place. Traveling over a flat tundra is much easier than traversing a mountainous, or hilly region.

Prep Like You Mean It

The first order of business is to make the decision to take prepping seriously. If prepping is something you have viewed as an interesting hobby, or an afterthought, then now would be a good time to get serious, get off the couch, and start grabbing gear. While knowledge and experience alone will provide you with some valuable insight on learning to take care of yourself, gear will allow you to put that knowledge to work.

Do Your Research & Gear Up

Conduct extensive research on bug-out bag designs and contents. Either find a prefabricated bug-out bag that has everything of importance, or purchase the equipment separately and assemble your own. You will need a bug-out bag for each individual in your family. Your bug-out bag should have enough essential supplies to allow you to survive in the wilderness for an isolated period of three days. The focus here should be on cost-effective, yet serviceable equipment. Do not cut corners on cost if the equipment you are purchasing isn't going to meet or exceed your needs. A dollar saved isn't worth the effort if the equipment fails when you need it most. Personally, I would recommend buying the gear separately and building your own bug-out bag(s). Ready-made bug-out bags may include items you don't want or need. When you purchase the gear individually, you can tailor your gear to your needs and preferences.

Remember, the bug-out bag, needs to be able to accommodate the survival gear you need, and you should be able to carry the fully loaded bug-out bag comfortably. Do not assume that you will be able to bug-out by vehicle if/when the time comes. A massive evacuation will clog all major avenues of escape. Make sure you can shoulder the pack and travel by foot over long distances without surrendering to early fatigue.

Practice Makes Perfect

When you buy gear, learn how to use it. Practice using it in your backyard if possible; get familiar with it. Once you feel comfortable handling it in a controlled environment, schedule an outing to practice using your gear in the wilderness, where your practice will be more beneficial by simulating a real world situation. If you do not practice with your gear, you aren't going to have much success surviving a simulated situation, let alone the reality of social collapse.

Chapter 2:
Plotting the Bug-Out Paths

Once you've assembled your gear, you need to establish a method of evacuating the area. This is going to depend largely on where you live, and the surrounding terrain, but there is some general advice to consider when plotting your bug-out path.

Map It

The first step in plotting bug-out paths is to acquire maps of the area you live in. You need as many maps as possible. Street maps of the given area will allow you to become familiar with the area's transportation routes. Topographical maps will indicate the various heights and depressions of the surrounding terrain. Neighborhood maps will give you more intimate details of your specific region. Underground maps of sewer and subway systems might also come in handy, especially if the social collapse situation involves closing down main arteries of above ground transportation.

Read It

You have to do more than just buy and store the maps. You need to be able to read them accurately. If you cannot learn this skill on your own, then consider registering for a map-reading course. You will also need a compass, whether or not you already know how to read the map, a compass is always an important piece of survival gear. By learning how to read a map and operate a compass, you will be able to plot alternative and unconventional routes of escape/evacuation.

Plot It

Study the maps intensively and plot out more than one back alley possibility. Identify primary routes as well as secondary. These paths can include above- ground departure, below-ground departure, or both. If you live in an urban/suburban area, the underground systems may be the only routes accessible to break beyond the perimeter of the city. Obviously nobody wants to actually crawl down in a sewer system to seek safety, but if that's the only option available, an understanding of how the system is positioned beneath the city will be a godsend.

Color-code It

Your bug-out paths should be color-coded to prevent

confusion. Alternate, secondary paths should stem from various locations off the primary path. Do not establish secondary paths from the primary path's same point of origin. If you do originate all secondary paths from the primary's origination point, you could find yourself wasting several valuable hours along various routes. If a primary route is inaccessible, you'll want to backtrack as little as possible before embarking in a different direction.

For those living in rural regions, or sprawling suburban settings, all of the above applies to you as well; however, you may have advantages over those living in metropolitan and compact suburban settings. Rural regions are usually ripe with two tracks and logging trails. ATV's, or other off-road vehicles, might still serve a purpose for the rural resident. Horses, bikes, and animal-drawn carriages, are also still common modes of transportation in these areas and may give you a faster method of evacuating than traveling by foot. Nonetheless, you still need to have your maps and be able to read them.

Isolate Yourself

The primary objective of plotting bug-out paths is to evacuate/escape an area, usually undetected. If you are following the crowd to a common location, you're headed for social collapse instead of away from it. The last thing you want to do is attempt to use familiar routes of travel, or interact with unfamiliar members of the community.

Social collapse makes everyone in the area a possible

target, so the less people know about your bug-out plans, the better. Granted, some people engage in a survival community concept, so they should share common locations for assembling, yet have alternate methods of getting there. Depending on the circumstances, a large group of like-minded survivalists all gathering together in the public eye, and heading in a different direction, is likely to draw unwanted attention and possibly make the group a target by criminals, or by government personnel. If you are going to share your bug-out plans and paths with anyone, they should either be living with you, or within reasonable range of the planned upon destination.

Use Alternative Methods of Transport

When studying the maps, look for all alternate routes of evacuation/escape. Depending on location and circumstances, waterways should be given consideration. The majority of people evacuating the area, rural or urban, are not going to be well-prepared survivalists. They are going to attempt to travel by conventional means and add to the confusion, chaos, and clogging of the transportation infrastructure. If you have personal watercraft, this might present a less common means of getting out of dodge before the rest of society figures out it's too late.

Practice Your Paths

You might also plot your bug-out paths and travel them to prepare and mark them in the event of social collapse. In rural communities this is not a very difficult process. Land surveyor's tape can be tied off to objects along your selected route, hatchet marks can be hacked into trees along the way. In a metropolitan, or urban area, this might be a little more difficult. You may have to use your imagination. You could attach identifiable flyers to street lamps or other objects along the route. You will undoubtedly want to revisit these identification marks in an urban area, as they have a tendency to be removed or covered up.

Strategically Stash Your Gear

Depending on what's available along your travel routes, you might want to consider stashing some of your gear, or supplemental supplies, in strategic locations, ensuring that you can retrieve the items if/when needed. Hiding your stash well will also eliminate the possibility of someone else stumbling across it. These are your survival safety deposit boxes. This concept is not mandatory when developing your bug-out paths, but it does have some benefits worthy of considering.

Maintaining a low profile is important to bugging-out. Slipping through the cracks, so to speak. If you leave your home with a bug-out bag loaded to the brim, you could be painting a target on your back. By strategically mapping out and stashing gear/supplies along various routes, you can vacate the area much quicker with less weight, without having to worry about whether or not you have everything. As you come across survival stashes, you can add them to your gear and soldier on. This will reduce fatigue and panic, as you race to safety.

Strategic staging of supplies will also allow you to bug-out from any given location, carrying the bare minimum in your bug-out pack. With a fully loaded bug-out bag, you either have to stash it in a close and convenient location on a daily basis, or it must be stationed in a specific spot for easy retrieval. This poses a problem for some survivalists, as they either have to carry it and store it daily, or hope they can get back to it should SHTF while they are away. The younger generation seldom leaves the house without carrying a backpack of some sort, so it wouldn't be difficult for them to assemble a similar style bag to carry daily, while loading up on previously planted supplies and gear along the way.

Chapter 3:
Where Are We Headed?

The final step of plotting bug-out path involves having a destination. This destination can be a temporary solution, or permanent. This is something you need to address personally when it comes to surviving a social collapse.

Temporary Shelter

If all you have is a temporary solution, then it will likely be necessary for you to relocate and build a shelter from time to time. Choosing this temporary solution will give you a little more freedom to make a decision on where to establish a permanent survival shelter after the dust settles. With a temporary shelter bug-out plan, you have the possibility of establishing several primary bug-out paths from various points of origin. For instance, you can plot four or five primary routes, heading in different directions, using your house as one point of origin and your place of business as a second point of origin. This increases your chances of getting out of the area.

Permanent Shelter

With permanent shelters, all primary and secondary routes of escape are going to be focused in one general direction. This eliminates the possibility of escaping to any of the remaining directions of the compass. That's not to say that permanent off-grid survival shelters don't have advantages. Quite the contrary; they have several advantages if they can be reached safely.

Permanent shelter solutions can be stocked with the necessary supplies/gear to provide long-term survival. Temporary shelters do not have this luxury. With a temporary shelter, and a three-day supply of essentials in your bug-out bag, you must have a plan in place for augmenting what supplies you've exhausted.

Isolate or Congregate

In a social collapse setting, you also have the option of flying solo or bringing along a group. In the latter case, your off-grid shelter must accommodate those with whom you've planned to escape. Refrain from picking up strays along the way, as they won't have the supplies to sustain themselves for long-term survival and your stored supplies will rapidly deplete. They are also strangers and therefore untrustworthy; even more so given the circumstances.

The decision you make about isolation or congregation will dictate what actions you take in the next phase of social collapse survival.

Chapter 4:
Temporary and Permanent Shelter Survivors

Temporary Shelter Survivors

Learn How to Forage, Filter, and Flourish

If you've chosen a temporary shelter, it will be necessary to know how to identify, forage, and harvest wild edibles familiar to the region. You will also need to have the skills to start a fire and keep it going. The food, water, and other supplies in your bug-out bag will disappear before you know it. Chances are, after three days' time, you won't be able to loot a grocery store, as they will already have been ransacked and left empty. You'll need to know how to collect, filter, and purify various forms of non-potable water to make it suitable for human consumption.

Live Off-the-beaten Path

You are going to want to find a setting that is off-the-beaten path and can't be easily identified from a distance. You will more than likely be traveling alone, either as a single person, a couple without kids, or a small family of four to five. Your safety and security will depend on how invisible you remain. Larger throngs of unprepared survivors and criminal elements will attack smaller well-supplied groups with impunity.

Protect Yourself

You are going to want to bring along personal protection in the form of suitable firearms. Knives, pistols, and shotguns will be easier to carry and use in a close quarters environment, which is the most likely scenario under these situations.

Permanent Shelter Survivors

Normalcy

For those who've made it to their permanent off-grid survival shelter, getting back to a sense of normalcy will be the first order of business. You'll need to unpack any additional items you've brought along, become familiar with the new surroundings, and complete any immediate tasks with relation to the shelter itself.

Getting an off-grid energy system up and running will consume some of your time, as will doing a perimeter check to ensure everything is in order. Ensuring that the compound hasn't been discovered/compromised in anyway will require some time and effort.

Set Ground Rules

Revisiting discussions about living at the permanent survival shelter should be reviewed, so that everyone is on the same page and realizes this is actually happening. Set duties, tasks, chores, and ground rules.

Go to Work

Ensuring that everything is in working order and ready to roll will be the primary focal point for permanent residents. If the off-grid survival location consists of a community style complex, then the first day should involve taking care of personal shelters, and scheduling an adult meeting for the following day to get things under way.

Chapter 5:
Living off the Land

Should a social collapse of national magnitude occur, it will once again be necessary to live off the land. The need to rely on nothing but ourselves and our skill sets will be crucial to survival. Even if some form of traditional infrastructure is still in existence – breadlines and soup kitchens, for instance – those that can fend for themselves, raise livestock and crops, will enjoy a much healthier lifestyle.

Raise Livestock & Crops

If you have a permanent survival shelter setting, then consider investing in raising livestock and crops to supplement your food supply. This can include farming large or small livestock and growing traditional crops. You can also investigate other methods of growing crops and keeping livestock, if you have off-grid energy equipment, such as aquaponics or hydroponics.

Hunt & Trap, Fish & Forage

For both temporary and permanent shelter survivors, hunting, trapping, fishing, and foraging for wild edibles will be necessary skill sets to learn proficiently. There are several problems that could come up when raising your own livestock or crops, so having the ability to secure what you need through other means is absolutely necessary.

Live Off the Land

Nature has provided everything required to sustain life for millions of years. It will provide us with almost everything we need in a modern day social collapse, as long as we familiarize ourselves with the right skill sets. Most people believe that living off the land is impossible, when in fact less than a century ago, more people lived off the land than in cities, and all of their produce and meat came from local farms, owned and operated by families. Commercialism and consumerism have obliterated the landscape and subliminally brainwashed today's citizens into dependency. This makes our reliance on conventional living conditions a recipe for disaster should serious social collapse occur.

You should familiarize yourself with growing your own

crops and raising livestock, even if it's just on a small scale. A few caged rabbits, and a window-sill herb garden, are enough to get you started with learning the intricacies of growing and raising your own.

Hunting, fishing, trapping, and foraging are all skills you can begin developing long in advance of ever needing them. Don't pick and choose a couple skill sets from this list and neglect the rest. Whatever your dietary habits may be – whether you're a carnivore, herbivore, or omnivore – when the SHTF, you'll want to take advantage of every possible source of protein and nutrition that presents itself. Every missed opportunity to put a meal on the table could be your last. So learn how to succeed at them all.

Finding water will be imperative. Regardless of how you choose to bug-out and where you decide to go, you are going to need water. The majority of natural water resources are not fit for human consumption, so you will need to purchase or learn how to build water purification and filtration devices.

Chapter 6:
The New Economic Format

In a serious large-scale social collapse, our currency system is probably not going to be of much use. People can't eat money, and it really has no significant value when everything else around you has crumbled to the ground. Bartering and trading will once again be the economic format by which we function in the aftermath of chaos. Coins, precious metals, gems, and jewelry may still have some value, but that value will not be reflected in stock market systems and will rely on the individuals participating in the transaction.

Value in Items & Skill Sets

You will need items, or valuable skill sets, to offer in

order to enter into any transaction with the hopes of making a deal. Having ammunition, or the skills and equipment necessary to offer reloading shells, would be a good idea. Not only will you be able to use surplus for bartering, but you'll be able to ensure that you never run out of a valuable asset in a survival situation. In this type of survival situation, anything and everything survival related will have a value affixed to it.

Be Ready to Labor

In social collapse, wage-earning jobs will likely be a thing of the past. Hard labor itself can be used as a viable item for bartering, and may be something you need to consider as part of your bug-out plan. It goes without saying that not everyone involved in the realm of survival has completed their entire bug-out plan. Social collapse could occur at any stage of preparation. If we haven't yet assembled the goods, gear, and supplies we need for long term survival, we may find ourselves trading the sweat from our brow for a few square meals here and there.

Trade, Services, and Bartering

Livestock and crops will be hot commodities and will require additional protection. When the SHTF and people are at the point of starvation, they will loot more than the local grocery store; they will rummage through fields foraging for anything ripe, and steal any livestock they can. Depending on where you are, what you raise, and the reproductive/growth cycles of your animals and produce, farming would be an extremely valuable asset to have when it comes time to bartering for things you want/need.

Being able to provide other services will help you carve a niche in the new economic market. With the absence of power and other conventional grid services, manually-operated farming equipment will be necessary. People who survive the first couple of months will need to clear land for planting their own crops, either individually or as a community. If you are the only one with the equipment and wherewithal to help, then you have a monopoly and can basically set your own price.

Gold, Silver, Precious Metals

Gold, silver, and other precious metals, gems and jewelry might also play an important role in re-establishing an economic system and assessing the value of the market. Then again, people can't eat metal or gemstones, so some may see these items as nothing more than bright shiny objects.

Haggling

One thing is certain, the new economic system, will involve haggling over the terms of the transaction, so learn how to be an effective salesperson. Fair Market Value will be a term no longer used. Supply, demand, and proper timing will net you the best return on the trade market. Keep what you have until the time is right and the demand is at its highest, then offload it for a larger profit than you would have earned when the supply was high and the demand was low.

Isolationist Self-sufficiency

Now, if you are operating a completely self-sufficient survival shelter, then investing in the local economy may not appeal to you. The establishment of this type of self-sufficient isolationist lifestyle is generally difficult for most modern-day Americans. We've been indoctrinated into believing that all of our goods and products come from Wal-Mart and other big box stores. The fact is they don't. Becoming completely self-reliant is not impossible. If you have relatives that currently live on an old farming homestead, go visit them. They may not be completely off-the-grid, but they live in a way that early settlers did, and not only do they survive, they flourish.

Chapter 7:
Establishing Energy

Off-grid energy is always a huge issue when it comes to discussing these types of alternatives for long-term survival. It is not impossible to live without electricity, running water, central air and heat, or conventional sewage systems. We have become so dependent on these services we wholeheartedly accept the misinformation that without power we shall perish. These components of modern day infrastructure are relatively new concepts along the timeline of human history. A number of retired Americans will regale you with stories of their early childhood living on the farm without lights, sharing an outhouse, and hand pumping water from a well. These stories didn't happen all that long ago.

Off-grid Energy

There are several off-grid methods of generating power. Wind, hydro, solar, and geothermal are the most commonly mentioned options. Steam power is a manual labor method that some survivalists include in their survival plans. Pedal-power platforms are beginning to gain headway as well.

As with everything, there are advantages and disadvantages associated with a number of these off- grid energy solutions. What you elect to use will depend on what natural elements, and/or personal preferences you have.

Wind

If wind is not a prevalent part of the local weather pattern, this type of off-grid energy solution isn't going to be worth the investment. If you do have plenty of wind, you will need to know how to provide maintenance to the system, and/or replace/repair any components that require attention. Winters can wreak havoc on wind turbines, and on the unprepared operator. Large chunks of ice can build up on the system, adding to the load bearing weight of the fan blades. These huge blocks of ice can also dislodge unexpectedly and come flying off the blades, posing dangerous potential for damage and destruction.

Solar

Solar power works well during clear sunny days. It isn't

very effective during the evening hours, or on dark overcast cloudy days, which are very common during winter months in northern tier states. Solar cells are expensive to purchase, as well as repair and replace.

Hydro

Hydro equipment requires naturally running water in order to generate power. Think of old-fashioned water wheels, and you'll have an idea of what's involved. Modern day equipment is quite different from the antique water wheel houses, but it still requires constant natural running water. In colder climates during winter, water can freeze or sheet over, which could pose problems for this type of gear. If the water supply is a large enough river, it could be used or dammed up by someone further upstream, again posing a problem for those downstream. This equipment also requires maintenance, replacement or repair, so having spare parts and knowledge will be necessary.

Geothermal

Geothermal units are power-generating devices that are buried. These might be great ideas for off-grid survival, but should they require maintenance or repair procedures, they will normally have to be unearthed entirely to repair the problem and restore the system. They also need to be buried to an appropriate depth depending on the seasonal habits of the region in which they are installed.

Manually-operated

Manually-operated off-grid power providers, such as steam engines and pedal platforms, do produce adequate power under the right conditions. But those conditions require physical labor; either shoveling coal, hauling and inserting logs into the fire, or pedaling the stationary bike platform to convert labor to energy.

Electricity would definitely make life in the aftermath of social collapse easier, but it is not essential to survival. All things considered it is a luxury, not an absolute necessity. Millions of people around the world currently live without power; some of them have never even encountered an electric device. They continue to thrive and survive by adhering to the traditions of their ancestors. If they can accomplish this, so can we.

Chapter 8:
Self Defense

In a social collapse scenario, self-defense is another absolute necessity. You may not like firearms, or even own one at the moment, but you may require one in a social collapse scenario. Do some research and find one suitable for your body frame then learn how to use it proficiently. It really doesn't matter what your personal opinions are in regards to guns. When it comes to social collapse, those with guns aren't going to care about your philosophies and ideals...and neither are their guns. Should things become aggressive, gun toters will have the upper hand in any confrontation.

Handguns & Shotguns

Consider handguns and shotguns for personal short-range self-defense, and rifles for long-range self-defense and/or hunting. You can supplement your firearms with other social collapse self-defense skills and gear; but if you neglect to include a firearm, all other investments may be for naught.

Martial Arts & Military Maneuvers

Martial arts are always an excellent secondary option for survival-related self-defense situations, as these methods tend to focus on close quarters hand-to- hand combat, which is an all too real possibility in a social collapse.

Knowing how to practice tactical armed military maneuvers will also assist you in social collapse conditions, especially if you have a large survival group with people old enough and responsible enough to handle weapons. Knowing and understanding these tactics can also aid you should Martial Law be part of the militarized response of law enforcement and government troops.

Take self-defense seriously when discussing social collapse. The law enforcement that may have been present beforehand will either be involved in some meaningless task to try and quell the massive civil upheaval, or they will be part of the force sent in to bring chaos back to order. You cannot assume that you will be able to rely on them in their expected capacity to keep you safe. You can only rely on yourself, your gear, your skills, and your abilities to use them.

Chapter 9:
Important Prepper Documents

For short-term social collapse situations, such as was the case in New Orleans after Hurricane Katrina, packing your important documents in your bug-out gear will be crucial. Birth certificates, personal identification cards, immunization records, property deeds and titles, relevant insurance papers, and copies of medical records are all things you will want to bring along and keep in a safe dry place. These documents will be necessary should you decide to relocate to another city or state. They will also come in handy after the region begins to rebuild itself should you decide to stay and invest in your torn community.

Originals & Copies

Keep originals, and carry copies of all these important documents. Financial records, credit card statements, and bank statements may be necessary in order to access your accounts from a satellite branch. They may also be necessary in order to file claims against an establishment should your financial portfolio be compromised.

In a Martial Law situation, ID cards may be demanded by controlling forces to document who you are, and where you were last seen or traveling. They may be required to pass certain checkpoints, or to leave or enter specific areas. On the flip side of that, ID cards will make it easier for controlling forces to identify you and document where you have been relocated to, so you may not always want to carry them on your person, especially if you are trying to sneak through the system and make it to your safe haven.

CONCLUSION

Social collapse conditions will require you to bug-out to seek shelter and fend for yourself, at least until the dust has settled and a small posse can scout out the surrounding area to determine how many others have survived, and under what conditions. For long-term social collapse conditions, you might want to consider bugging-out to a safe haven and staying put for a period of at least a month, if not longer.

Plenty of criminal activity is bound to occur, and until order has been restored, mass pockets of the population should be avoided. A small, covert capable scouting posse should be sent forth to examine all surrounding areas and identify other survival outposts or conditions within cordoned-off areas, if possible.

Depending on the circumstances and the information provided by the scouting party, a decision should be made whether to stay put, under-the-radar, or reach out to other survival groups and communities to engage in rebuilding the area. A third option is to develop a larger plan of action to counteract the event of social collapse and return to a more comfortable and convenient lifestyle.

As we stated earlier, social collapse can be small-scale or large-scale. As events continue to unfold in the Middle East, the situation involving international interests could have globally epic ramifications. Oil prices could skyrocket overnight, and shortages would drive the price of gas through the roof. This will have a domino effect throughout the infrastructure of all societies involved. Industrial food suppliers would have to raise their prices to compensate for the rise in gas prices, as it would cost them more to deliver, and they aren't about to lose money.

Grocery stores would have to roll back on what they carry in stock, as prices escalate and people begin reserving their spending habits to things of vital importance for survival.

Mass transit systems will also raise their prices to compensate for the higher cost of operation. They will likely have to reduce scheduled runs in order to remain profitable, which will have an enormous impact on those suffering economically, as many will need to rely on mass transit to save on transportation costs. State or federal government agencies may issue fuel ration cards, making it all but impossible to consider traveling, taking a vacation, or simply running errands.

Employers here in America are not going to raise wages for their employees overnight to compensate for the astronomical rise in the cost of living. Eventually food shortages will follow, as will the reduction, or rationing, of conventional grid services, such as running water, sewage, electricity, and heat. Sooner or later, this is going to cause a fracture in society in which people begin to revolt, either through peaceful or violent protest.

Should things arrive at the point where people are spilling into the street either to evacuate, escape, or protest violently, you'll need to be as far away from the scene as possible. In the early stages of a social collapse, there will be too many unknowns. Do not stick around to find out what might or might not happen. Leave immediately and make your way to safety. Account for everyone in your party, and after the predetermined length of stay has been met, scout out the area. Don't show your hand before you have to. Take care of yourself and family first, worry about others after the dust has settled, and don't stray from the program. In other words, stick to your plan unless you can be absolutely sure that normalcy and the Rule of Law have been re-established.

ALL RIGHTS RESERVED. No part of this publication may be reproduced or transmitted in any form whatsoever, electronic, or mechanical, including photocopying, recording, or by any informational storage or retrieval system without express written, dated and signed permission from the author.

DISCLAIMER AND/OR LEGAL NOTICES: Every effort has been made to accurately represent this book and it's potential. Results vary with every individual, and your results may or may not be different from those depicted. No promises, guarantees or warranties, whether stated or implied, have been made that you will produce any specific result from this book. Your efforts are individual and unique, and may vary from those shown. Your success depends on your efforts, background and motivation.

The material in this publication is provided for educational and informational purposes only and is not intended as medical advice. The information contained in this book should not be used to diagnose or treat any illness, metabolic disorder, disease or health problem. Always consult your physician or health care provider before beginning any nutrition or exercise program. Use of the programs, advice, and information contained in this book is at the sole choice and risk of the reader.

www.ingramcontent.com/pod-product-compliance
Lightning Source LLC
Chambersburg PA
CBHW071256280526
45788CB00004B/1735